Animals in Danger

By Sean McCollum

Illustrated by Sam Valentino

Library For All Ltd.

LIBRARY FOR ALL

DIGITAL EDUCATION · FOR THE WORLD

Library For All is an Australian not for profit organisation with a mission to make knowledge accessible to all via an innovative digital library solution. Visit us at libraryforall.org

Animals in Danger

This edition published 2022

Published by Library For All Ltd
Email: info@libraryforall.org
URL: libraryforall.org

USAID FROM THE AMERICAN PEOPLE

Original illustrations by Sam Valentino

Animals in Danger
McCollum, Sean
ISBN: 978-1-922835-33-8
SKU02726

Animals in Danger

Liberia is a beautiful country with many wild animals. Birds sing in the forest. Monkeys climb in the trees. Forest elephants take baths in the rivers.

However, some animals are in danger. People cut down the trees where they live. Hunters shoot them for food. Sadly, some of these animals are disappearing.

Pygmy hippos

Liberia is one of the few places in Africa where pygmy hippos live. They look like regular hippos but are smaller. They are also very shy. They usually move around at night.

Pygmy hippos live in the forest, but they spend a lot of time in water. It helps them stay cool. They search for plants and fruit to eat on land.

Diana monkeys

There are different kinds of monkeys in the world. Liberia has the Diana monkey. Its fur is black, white and brown.

Diana monkeys live in groups. They stay near the tops of trees, where they hunt for fruit and insects. Living together helps them stay safe. They call to each other if there is danger.

Forest elephants

African elephants are very big and like grassy areas. The elephants in Liberia stay in the forests. They are called forest elephants. They look like African elephants, but they are smaller. A baby elephant is called a calf.

Forest elephants live in family groups. They walk together among the trees. They use their long trunks to pick fruit and leaves to eat.

Leopards

Leopards are big cats that live in many parts of Africa. They have yellow and brown fur covered with black spots. Their babies are called cubs.

Leopards are very strong and great hunters. They rest during the day and hunt at night. They catch antelopes, monkeys, and other animals.

Pangolins

Pangolins are also called "scaly anteaters". Their hard scales, made from the same material that forms human hair and nails, keep them safe.

Pangolins are the same size as cats. They have powerful claws to rip up nests and long sticky tongues to slurp up termites and ants. They roll themselves into balls when they are threatened.

African manatees

Some rivers in Liberia are home to African manatees. They are grey, and their tails look like paddles. Their tails and front flippers help them swim.

African manatees eat plants. Sometimes, they eat fish and clams, too. They sleep during the day and move around at night.

Wild animals need places to live. Liberia's forests help protect them.

Sapo National Park is a special place in Liberia. Wild animals are safe there. The trees cannot be cut down. No hunting is allowed. Caring for places such as the Sapo National Park helps wild animals, so they do not disappear.

SAPO NATIONAL PARK

Our Heritage. Our future.

WELCOME
WE HOPE YOU ENJOY
YOUR VISIT

4km →

You can use these questions to talk about this book with your family, friends and teachers.

What did you learn from this book?

Describe this book in one word. Funny? Scary? Colourful? Interesting?

How did this book make you feel when you finished reading it?

What was your favourite part of this book?

download our reader app
getlibraryforall.org

About the contributors

Library For All works with authors and illustrators from around the world to develop diverse, relevant, high quality stories for young readers. Visit libraryforall.org for the latest news on writers' workshop events, submission guidelines and other creative opportunities.

Did you enjoy this book?

We have hundreds more expertly curated original stories to choose from.

We work in partnership with authors, educators, cultural advisors, governments and NGOs to bring the joy of reading to children everywhere.

Did you know?

We create global impact in these fields by embracing the United Nations Sustainable Development Goals.

libraryforall.org

www.ingramcontent.com/pod-product-compliance
Lightning Source LLC
Chambersburg PA
CBHW040319050426
42452CB00018B/2930